D1196069

Both and All
by Sarah Auna

Published in the United States
by Sarah Auna
2545 Fernbrook Ln N
Plymouth, MN 55447

ISBN: 979-8-218-10892-2

Audio ISBN: 979-8-218-10891-5

Library of Congress Control Number: 2022921770

I dedicate this book to Eleanor and Eddie.
I love you more than a middle schooler loves lip gloss,
more than a 10-year-old loves skateboarding.
Thanks for choosing me.
I love you, both and all.

CONTENTS

FRAY

In the magic moment
when the ginkgos let themselves go
– all at once and completely –
we were walking.
I thought it was fortune; it was
foreshadowing.

I knew it was over
when you came home;
nails freshly polished (yellow)
the first and second fingers of your right hand
shaped into long, sharp talons.

In the end all you could say,
was as sure as you were you loved me,
you're sure now you don't.

You read our vows
and you just don't feel the
same way you once did.

I regret I didn't know
your understanding of vows
before this moment.

When people ask, I'll tell them
you were too sick
to be married anymore.

This is truer than divorce.
This is kinder than the truth.

It tracks I feel pride
when I say you were my wife…
even though the letters
"e" and "x"
precede it.
You always were an alchemist.

It's like you died,
which might have been easier,
because then love would still be living.

You told the truth
that first Christmas
when you wrote,
"I want to do life with you. Simple, beautiful life."
You did want to do life with me,
but only when it was simple,
beautiful.

When your devotion left
it was like the hush
of the first snow.

Cold.
Audible.
Undeniable.

A sign of the season's change.

I wanted to show you
the first draft of my vows.

Have a baby with you,
raise a child.

At the very least,
play a few more
records.

I was still moved by the sound
of my name on your lips,
even when you used it to tell me
to leave.

There's nowhere I wouldn't
have gone for you.
Including away.
So, I did.

The thing you dislike the most about me
is how much I like you.

You couldn't talk me out of loving you.
So you talked yourself out of loving me instead.

Grief is when my body
reminds me of your body.
It's feeling once so seen
by someone I can no longer
bear the sight of.

It's too much for one body.
So I stir my grief into soups and scones
and ask my loved ones
to eat it.

I gave you
my favorite
poems
songs
flowers
scents.

I lost them all
in the divorce.

I learned to lick a pussy in the most devotional way.
Slow.
Wide.
Every stroke of the tongue,
an uppercase "L"
for
LOVE
LOVE
LOVE

She lives in my memory,
a myth of extremes.
Her wonder proportionate
with her ability to wound.

Both and All

Both and all
is what you promised
when I asked you to be
my lover and wife.

Both and all
is what you broke
when I gave you
my heart and family.

Both and all
is what you desired
when I asked you
fingers or tongue?

Both and all
is what you returned
when you
handed back my life.

Both and all
is what you welcomed
when I offered you
comfort for your pain.

Thank you.
Fuck you.
Both and all.
~~~

UNDONE

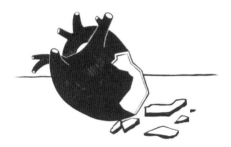

The Last Time

I carry myself across the threshold of our front door
I know this will be the last time
I understand this place as home.

Fingers brush across the couch
where we fit – just so.
Plus a kid
or two
or three.

Thumb the titles in our record bin,
I'll only take the ones
belonging to my Dad.

Put on one more kettle,
and look at all the mugs.
Pack the ones
with the right balance of
sentimentality, hand and mouthfeel.

Shuffle past the dog hair
–some of which will make the move–
avoiding the creaky floorboards.
It's still mine, this empty house,
but my body behaves
like she doesn't want
anyone to know I'm here.

Glance around our bedroom,
I can tell the time of day by the shadow play
and neighborhood sounds.

My eyes land on our bookshelf
and I begin to slide covers
backs and bindings
away from one another.
Unmingling our books
feels like ripping flesh from bone.

"I'm sorry," I whisper
to the hand-inscribed titles
I'll be leaving behind.

The last thing I do
before I go
is lay down in our bed
and take a photo of myself,
visibly bruised.
A place of worship, no more.

~~~

Now I know why
you never put up pictures
of loved ones
in your home.

How many people did we joyfully
tell our love story to?
That's how many hearts you've broken.

You told me to stay in my lane,
so you could make a quick exit.

The cost of entry
to your sanctuary was silence.
I was only invited
if I promised to stay small
and leave my needs
at the door.

I didn't
leave you.
You insisted
I (we)
stop showing up to
my (our)
life.

You refused to say
"wasted time"
as a promise
to a dying friend.

We honored him (and you)
by refusing to say it too.

Your words kept your promise
but your body didn't.

It's the same way you kept your vows.

What a thing,
that you were contemplating
my eviction
while I was contemplating
my cremation.
"As long as my ashes
are scattered
in our flower garden,"
I said.

.

You will be
my peony love.
BIG
alluring
bountiful
and fleeting.
Dead overnight,
in the grandest gesture
of surrender.

You can control me
or love me.
Pick one.

You can control yourself
or love yourself.
Pick one.

It's easier
to control
a narrative
than it is
to control
a person.

You
chose
control
over
love;
fixing
over
feeling.

Unaccountable:
there's a problem,
but you've wrapped it in a
"you're the problem"
package.

When you're the most comfortable suffering
and you're best in chaos,
you will create the conditions needed to "flourish."

1

Having matching tattoos is irrelevant,
you left a much more permanent mark.

2

It's unbearable
that the change of address stickers
are waiting for me in my mailbox
for an entire year.
A daily reminder of ruin.

3

You can keep
the pictures of me
you saved in your
"hidden album"
You took all of me anyhow.

Wedding Day

The truth is our wedding day is still one
of the best days of my entire life.
We carried dahlias, carrot fronds and
gingkos grown at home.
When we planted them,
we thought we were growing flowers
we were actually growing bouquets.

I wore the lace shawl you bought for me
on our fifth date
because you already knew, even then.
Your dress? Hand painted in strokes of
pink, green and ochre.
You serenaded me with songs we loved,
and I you, with words that mattered.

Even now, my vows to you and the children
are some of the best words I've ever written.
We recited them so tenderly,
including a secret vow
you whispered into my ear alone.

It was a ceremony in the round,
and we were encased by our loved ones
who were holding their hearts in their
hands, and their breath,
because the wedding came as quickly as
one season of flowers.
My goodness, what a peak season it was.

~~~

The Vows You Actually Kept

Today, you are setting your intention toward one another.
But, over time, you will distance yourself
by rejecting love and refusing to trust.
Yes?

"That's right."

Each of us is free to change and grow
and you promise to gaslight your wife
if this growth or change
interferes with your control of the family.
Can you?

"I can."

In daily life, you will twist
needs, words, and concerns
to paint a picture
that will not allow anyone to be fully seen,
especially yourself.
Will you?

"I will."

In moments you feel vulnerable or less-than,
you will build an emotional vault so thick,
there will be no light or community allowed in.
No one will be able to see you
in this darkness.
Is this true?

"It is."

When conflict arises,
you will auto-pilot through it
using the social work skills
you acquired in college.
Will you?

"I will."

When you are suffering,
you will minimize it.
When you see the other is suffering,
you will acknowledge it
as long as it doesn't require an apology from you.
Can you?

"I can."

You will remember that each person
is doing the best they can
with what they have
and you will use this as an excuse
to shirk responsibility over
and over
and over
again.
Is this true?

"It's true."

Your relationship is adjacent to
the single-family-home
you've built for you and your son.
It's a place you can choose to visit
when things are pleasant
or if it looks like you could be a hero.
Is this right?

"That's right."

You want to be married
but you've been ignoring so many hurts
for so long
it will only be possible for a short time.
You have decided the person standing in
front of you
is the best person for you
as long as she is obedient and ignores
her intuition.
Yes?

"Sure thing"

Repeat after me…

"I take you to be something other than
yourself.
I will love some select parts of you,
trusting no others.
I will question your integrity
and feel disgusted by
your love for me.
I choose none other than
Sarah to be my wife."

"For now."

~~~

I wanted
to do the work
of changing.

You wanted
to do the work
of staying the same.

I was standing in the street
a grate at my feet
full of leaves and debris and brokenheartedness.

My friend asked if she could pray for me
and I felt myself hollow at the deep vulnerability
of accepting such a gift.

I expected her to ask for
Reunion!
Resolution!
Reconciliation!

"Break it all open!" she said.

In doing so, she raised the volume
on a bell I had already heard ringing;
Undeniable truth flooded my heartbody.
It was already so.

There's nothing
in my new space
that reminds me of you;
I wouldn't allow it.
Except…
one drop of your blood
left on a set of sheets
we never fucked on;
these are the two reasons
I allowed them
to come along at all.

THROUGHLINE

It's important to know
how uninterested
some people are
in relief.

How much someone is loved,
is no match
for how unsafe they feel
in their body.

If I want to stop bleeding,
I need to stop throwing myself against
your barricades.

If I want to be heard and seen,
I need to stop showing up at your
fortress.

Essentials for Leaving a Marriage

A kettle for coffee or tea
or any kind of witch's brew
(it's a traveling cauldron)

Cotton everything
(because you'll need to breathe on all levels)

Thigh rescue lotion
(Lord knows there's already enough friction)

Tax documents
(finances are about to get as thick as those thighs)

Any of the following books
(read them or clutch them):

Untamed
by Glennon Doyle

When Things Fall Apart
by Pema Chödrön

The Four Agreements
by don Miguel Ruiz

And a vibrator (for when feeling returns)

How do I care without carrying? How do I ca
ng? How do I care without carrying? How do
arrying? How do I care without carrying? How
out carrying? How do I care without carrying?
ithout carrying? How do I care without carryi
without carrying? How do I care without carr
care without carrying? How do I care without
do I care without carrying? How do I care wit
How do I care without carrying? How do I ca
ng? How do I care without carrying? How do
arrying? How do I care without carrying? How
out carrying? How do I care without carrying?

I mistook one of my
greatest teachers,
for one of my
greatest loves.

One understanding of trauma
is too much, too fast, too soon.
If this is true,
then my love is yours
and your leaving, mine.

It's not that I couldn't handle it;
it's that I
Handled.
It.
All.

Sometimes it feels safe
to lay on my back again.
Heart, open.
Belly, soft.
Thighs, turned out.
Other times,
I'm forced to curl it all in.
My whole body, fist tight.
Protecting myself
against the memory
of the fight to be loved.

I refuse to have a fenced-off heart,
barbed with crystalized spikes of pain.
So when I drive past our old house
I open my hand and press my palm to the window.
Press my palm to the pain.

I send nothing but
love-love-love
to all the people,
all the ghosts still living there.

The ghosts still riding their bikes around the block
and sledding down the hill in winter.
Playing baseball in the diamond
and pushing through the soil as sedum.

All the ghosts still waiting, untouched,
at the front door of the house
you refused to call ours.

I poured it all out.
You held it all in.
Because of our dispositions,
the space between us
grew
too
great.

I'm stuck between wishing
I had more time to love you,
and knowing that loving you more
would have made it worse.

May I use this pain,
to propel me
toward my purpose.

May I allow this grief
to burden me so heavily
I sink
down
down
down
to the deepest dark
where the pearl
is waiting.

We knew how to be in love.
We didn't know how to be in life.

I hold a high vision for you,
It's what I've done all along.
Much higher than you held for yourself.
Much higher than you held for me.

I accept the nature of endings,
and have found some gutting and grace
in the letting go.
I'll do my best to see this time through
with ceremony.

Even if you couldn't give it to me,
there is healing
in a good
bye.

MEND

I am tenderized by the lesson of grief.
Intimate with the act of self-betrayal.
Fortified with the knowledge
that I will (try to) never do that to myself again.

Each new interaction, an invitation
to practice wisdom,
hard won.

All the
fated encounters,
green lights,
and magnetism
were designed
to guide me toward you
so I could learn
what I needed to learn.

It was still fated,
just not the outcome
I expected.

I am a career rescuer.
Comfort is my currency,
and I will pay and pay.

Care is my intention,
but depletion the outcome;
oftentimes,
for all.

I'm going to take all of this capacity for attunement
and apply it to my own subtle body.

The way I hold my mouth,
sense a soft spot in my belly
and cry with every orgasm.
I will become my own clues,
my own Nancy Drew.

For the Kids

I kneel down…
this is the right shape for the moment.

I'm sorry I was blinded by my own unmet needs
and couldn't see your little hands in the air;
in one a red flag and in the other, a white.

I'm sorry I let reckless enthusiasm
take the wheel
and drive all three of us
to a destination with no vacancy.

I'm sorry I used the slack from your resilience,
the false notion of childhood flexibility,
to make room for decisions that would
leave us brittle and frayed.

Does it feel safe to hand me your flags?
I'll learn to stitch them up into a quilt that
will wrap us up–three.

Graciously, you do.

I take your little palms in mine
and press them to my cheek–pink.
I try to explain
the only training for motherhood
is on-the-job;
a role which asks me to cross my own lines,
in order to know where the lines are.

I try to explain
the unspoken vow of motherhood,
which is to try.

To find out
what I need to find out
about my own joy and sorrow
and use it to fortify myself,
and my relationship
to everyone around me.

I try.

~~~

Your help is not always needed,
but your here-ness is.

Fix-it energy in you,
implies brokenness in others.

Try doing nothing, and do it well.

Allow, allow, allow.
They will find their way.

There is worth
in your presence
alone.

Beloved,

Keep some light for you.
Call it back into your bones.
Cure it into a concentrated honey,
that nourishes you first,
and is offered only upon invitation.
When they ask, and you allow,
a sweetly secured bond will form.
A hexagonal home
for love to live in.

Love,
Yourself

The Narrow Place

The reverberation of our own voices
bounce against the walls of the narrow place,
finding their way back to us.
We're saying what we need to hear.

Here, there's only room enough for words,
sounds that float on air
and find their way to our hearts,
by way of our ears.

Here, there's not enough space
to hold onto what was
and what will be
at the same time.

Here, we have gone so far in (or is it out?)
we must dissolve ourselves
in order to pass.

Here, such vulnerability demands
we allow ourselves to be formed
to the specifications of the narrow place
so we may expand
tender and new,
having endured
telling the truth
on ourselves.

~~~

We no longer cover one another
but your grandmother still watches over me;
Her presence is a light, spirited hummingbird.
And my grandmother still watches over you.
Her ashes feed the regal delphinium which
nods encouragingly in your garden.

On the mornings I shower
and it's just me
and whatever song my subconscious has sent me,
just me
and the relationship dynamic I'm
thoughtfully trying to make sense of,
just me
and the luminous soap bubbles playing
across my breasts in the 7:11 light,
just me
and my sweetly scented hair and neck,
on those mornings,
I am the woman of my dreams.

My big life impact plan:
Say "I love you"
as often as possible,
to as many people as possible.
Myself included.

My entire self concept changed
when I stopped seeing signs as
warnings,
and began to understand them as
confirmations.

When I started saying,
"Thank you,"
where I used to say,
"Sorry."

When I started to speak to myself
in the affirmative:
I have love
I give love
I am love.

Lessons Learned While Alone

I like to take care of other
people's troubles
so I don't have to face my own.

The internet can teach me how to whistle,
LOUDLY!
It will surprise and delight me
so sincerely, I will tip over with laughter and tears.

Those three guitar chords
I taught myself in college,
they'll always be in my fingers.

Books are like pizzas,
some are worth finishing
more than others.

Speaking of finishing,
multiple orgasms *are* a thing.

I want other people to feel better
so I can feel better, actually.

Nothing I ever thrift online will fit,
and I'm going to have big feelings about this.
So I learn about self regulation
and find a tailor.

Gardens I've lost will haunt me
just as much as the lovers.

So I'll thumb through the seed
library I lovingly curated in a past life
and make sense of what can be planted
in *this* season's soil.
Knowing no matter how deeply
I love their flowers,
some seeds will need to stay in storage
a while longer.

~~~

I want my writing and my motherhood,
my love and my life,
to be answers
to beautiful questions.

We're home.
We are home.
There is sanctuary here
for our delicate, honied hearts;
whose nectar was made by the bees and
the Dogwood trees.

On a hill, high enough for the sun's light
to shine from sunset to sunrise
and back again.

I listened to our love song tonight; all the way through.
It found me.
Totally.
Disarmed.
In the bathtub, drinking a beer
and sending pictures of my
soft shoulder to a new lover.

Brain said, "Nope, nope, nope."
Heart said, "Let's see where this goes?"

Tears fell and I waited
for the seizure of my middle body…
but I stayed soft
listening through a light veil of nostalgia.
And it hurt,
but not enough for me to harden.

Sorrow

Sorrow is your whole self,
groundless and consumed.
Uncontrolled, retching into a basket of
clean laundry.

I thought I had immunity.
I thought I'd be the only person
time couldn't heal.

But many months later,
I opened up Mary Oliver again,
to see if she uses periods at the end of her sentences.
Thumbed immediately to
"The Uses of Sorrow"
and she told me that someone she loved once
had given her a box full of darkness
and that this, too, was a gift.

OFFER

Ecstasy

Ecstasy
is your whole self,
sensual and authentic.
Held sweetly
by safety.

I thought I had it
all figured out–
who I was
and what I desired.

But it belonged
to someone else,
their dreams
their needs
their standards.

It wasn't until the dating app asked me,
"Do you prefer men or women?"
that I was baptized by my knowing.

Ecstasy,
she was waiting for me,
and when I came in,
I came out…
and came
and came
and came.

~~~

I met a woman with
my grandmother's lucky birthday.
She reminded me
everyone I meet is my destiny.

"We are good moms,"
we whisper
over wet lips
with wise, wide
tongues;
I wake with sticky fingers
every morning since I met you.
I want to take long, cool, gulps
from the fountain
of your mouth.
It hums one note,
two octaves.
Ecstasy and sorrow;
early and late;
freedom and foundation.

Oranges come in sections
so you can have a bite for yourself
and a bite for your lover
and bite to hold up to the golden
afternoon sun
and a bite to touch to her nipple
and a bite to
and a bite to
and a bite to

It's not always like this,
but some days
you can have it all.

Your heart,
broken and mended
three-times-over
by justice and music and sex.

Your calling,
is to reach for the moment
when it comes.

Hold it loosely with your sacred,
unclenched palms
and pray the one-and-ever-only
three-part prayer:
"Yes. Welcome. Thank you."

Good sex, like music,
pulls something out of your bones.

It rocks your hips,
unsolicited,
while you brush your teeth.
It compels you to reach for the towel
she dried her face on last night,
so you can press it to your mouth
this morning.

It's the kind of thing you'll carry
in your body for always.
The type of memory that might get you
all the way home from Wyoming.

I ask:
"Want to fall in love with me, together?"
"Want to fall in love with you, together?"

You respond:
"Everything is wanted for you and
nothing is asked."

So we hold one another (and ourselves)
long and close.
Enough that the pattern of my bra
leaves an impression of lace
across the skin of your beautiful breast.

Make love in the afternoon once in a while
and take in the way
the light touches your lover's face
and the space between your thighs.
Drink in the details,
usually covered by night.

Let me lick the sweat
from the deep curve
which runs parallel to your spine?

I want to dip my fingers into the sweet
space
that falls at the intersection
of your wide heart and deep hips.

The soft skin of your inner wrist
the tone of your strong legs
the subtle lift of your round nose.

May my lips
be so lucky
to know well
a body like yours.

You put words
to the unknown-most sensations of my heart.
The same way the tall grasses
show us the shape of the wind.

I want you to wet my fingers
'til my cupped palm fills
and runs down both sides of my wrist.

I want you to moan into my mouth
while you hold me,
laugh so hard our bellies clap;
little high-fives.

I want you to press your cheek against
my back
so when you breathe,
a circle of condensation forms.

I want you to snore into my hair while
we're sleeping
so it wakes me up
and I can know again
we're in one another's arms.

Your radiance, goodwill and heart
walk into the room
before you do.

A presence that precedes you,
by a few feet
on all sides.

You're the kind of woman
who makes me want to
take my rings off,
turn my ringer off,
take my clothes off.
But mostly,
my armor.

You, an
exuberant
golden honey
that washes overs me
right down to the center
of the center
of my
body.

This will end.
As all things do.

So we have made a commitment
to care for the end
as much as the beginning.

With a deep conversation; a joint.
Maybe some homemade applesauce
and complete respect for one another's
crumpled, hopeful hearts.

Be they the hearts beating in our smooth, tan chests,
or the hearts that will beat
under wrinkled, parchment skin.

I am the Lover of Mothers

I am the lover of mothers
I hold their bodies
their hands
their hopes

I am the lover of the lovers of mothers. Of
Moms and Vobs
of Abbas and Aunties
of Grandmas and Nanas and Omas.

I am the lover of creation bodies,
and the parents who love creation into being.

I hold their hips
and their hair
and their hurts.

I am the lover of mothers.
My lover is a mother.
I am a mother.

We hold one another.

We
Hold
Hold
Hold
Release.

~~~

I don't know much about motherhood
outside of what my children teach me.
But I do know when your child looks you
in the eye at 2 AM
and says, "You're a good one,"
you take that gift and let it fill
your whole past
your whole present
your whole future.

To All the Trees I've Loved

Jolene, an exuberant magenta crabapple
whose beauty was beyond compare,
the city ash, could never.

The ginkgo tree on State Street,
whose roots ran deep and down,
remaining true since the time of dinosaurs.
I tattooed one of your fallen fans,
and now carry you on the curve of my shoulder
everywhere I go.

The white pine
waving to me from the side of Hwy 35.
"Hi, friend!"
"Bye, friend!"
your boughs said to me
as I commuted from the Northland.

The single birch, who grew directly
toward the sun, unobstructed.
Your companions were cleared
so the Sunrisers could have
an unobstructed sight line.
You became the view.

A redbud tree, given to me as a gift.
Lugged, tugged, drug, dug and planted
days before this gardener was fired.
My friends tell me you didn't survive.
I, however, did.

To the Texas cypress
who dappled my ecstasy with
shade and shelter, a witness to bliss,
and bliss herself.

To the elder oaks who hold our home,
you wrap your branches around this nest.
So established are you it's clear,
we are on your land,
we are in your arms.

~~~

A Field Guide for my Daughter

My mother stayed the night last night.
I told her I wrote a book.
Her attentiveness and sacrifice are in it;
her worry is in there too.
The way she taught me to ask a
question, instead of stating a need;
my eyes, ears and heart always attuned
to someone outside of myself.
The way she taught me how to sit
with the brokenhearted
is the way I sit with myself now.
Thank you, Mom.

My grandmother visited me at sunset yesterday
I told her I wrote a book.
Her curiosity and flirtation are in it;
her secret-keeping is in there too.
The way she taught me to put my face on,
and never allow others to see my sores.
The way she taught me to check in on my people
is the way I check in with myself now.
Thank you, Grandma.

My great-grandmother met me
in a dream the other night
I told her I wrote a book.
The way she was abandoned by her
family and nicknamed "Bye" is in it;
her commitment to that family
even in chaos is in there too.
The way she birthed the most powerful
woman (my grandmother)
and lost her life doing so
is the way I birth myself now.
Thank you, Great Grandma.

My great-great Auntie hovers
above the waters of my life
I told her I wrote a book.
She raised Bye, and then raised Bye's baby,
when Bye died only 10 days into motherhood.
The way my Auntie whispered devotion
into my DNA is in it;
The way she whispered fear and
hyper-vigilance is in there too.
How she stepped into the fold
of other people's families
so that generations could unfurl
is my purpose now.
Thank you, Great-Great Auntie.

My daughter sat with me on the couch today
I told her I wrote a book.
A field guide to my heart and mannerisms.
My hurt and healing.
The way I rescue people from themselves is in it;
the way I destroy myself doing so is in there too.
How I am the first in four generations of women
who wasn't raised by a motherless mother,
and how like them I choose love
again and again and again.
Across the ages.
It's the inheritance I aim to leave her with,
an artifact handed from my heart to hers.

ACKNOWLEDGMENTS

Thank you to the brave gay poets who
wrote before me. The forever-editor of
my first book, Alex Wegman.
My visionary cover artist Bekah Worley.
Hannah Jensen, my graphic designer with
the most and the crew at Franklin Press.
To my sweetheart and muse Rachel Kurtz
who is a masterful co-writer and kisser.
To all my first readers, ancestors
and friends who believed me when
I told them a book was on the way.
To my therapist RB for holding the
flashlight and finally, to my parents,
it's all entirely because of your love.

ABOUT THE AUTHOR

Sarah (she/her) is a queer woman living on
occupied Dakota and Anishinaabe territory
(also known as Minneapolis).
She has had two children, two marriages,
and two divorces, all before 40.
A woman of passion, valor, and disruption,
Sarah has made a living through writing,
production, teaching, and birth advocacy.
She proudly proclaims that
Black Lives Matter, Love is Love,
and will always point out a beautiful shadow.